EELS

A Buddy Book by
Deborah Coldiron

ABDO
Publishing Company

UNDERWATER
WORLD

VISIT US AT
www.abdopublishing.com

Published by ABDO Publishing Company, 8000 West 78th Street, Edina, Minnesota 55439.

Coordinating Series Editor: Sarah Tieck
Contributing Editor: Michael P. Goecke
Graphic Design: Deborah Coldiron
Cover Photograph: Photos.com
Interior Photographs/Illustrations: Animals Animals - Earth Scenes: R. Jackman/OSF (page 17); Art Explosion (page 22); Clipart.com (pages 9, 30); Brandon Cole Marine Photography (pages 23, 28); ImageMix (pages 5, 23, 25, 29); Minden Pictures: Sue Daly/npl (pages 22, 23), Peter Verhoog/Foto Natura (page 19), Norbert Wu (pages 13, 20, 21); Photos.com (pages 5, 7, 11, 20, 23, 25, 27)

Library of Congress Cataloging-in-Publication Data

Coldiron, Deborah
    Eels / Deborah Coldiron.
      p. cm. — (Underwater world)
    Includes index.
    ISBN 978-1-59928-818-5
    1. Eels—Juvenile literature. I. Title.

QL637.9.A5C65 2007
597'.43—dc22
                                                        2007014850

Table Of Contents

The World Of Eels 4

Up Close And Personal 8

A Growing Eel 12

Getting Stronger 16

Eel Impostors 20

The Real McCoy 22

Dinner Hour 24

Enemy Territory 26

Fascinating Facts 28

Learn And Explore 30

Important Words 31

Web Sites 31

Index 32

The World Of Eels

Every living creature needs water. Some animals not only need water, they live in it, too.

Scientists have found more than 250,000 kinds of plants and animals living underwater. And, they believe there could be one million more! The eel is one animal that makes its home in this underwater world.

Seventy percent of Earth's surface is covered in water. Eels live in this underwater world.

Eels are found in freshwater and salt water around the world. There are more than 500 **species** of eels.

Eels are long, snake-shaped fish. Their skin is slimy and generally has no scales.

The smallest eels are about four inches (10 cm) long. The largest can reach about 12 feet (4 m) in length.

Eels often hide among rocks and coral on the ocean floor.

Up Close And Personal

Many types of eels swim in the world's waters. These include moray eels, snake eels, and conger eels. There are also freshwater eels, garden eels, and many other kinds.

Most eels have bodies designed to slither through small cracks in the seafloor. Unlike most fish, many eels do not have scales. Instead they have smooth, slimy skin.

The Body Of An Eel

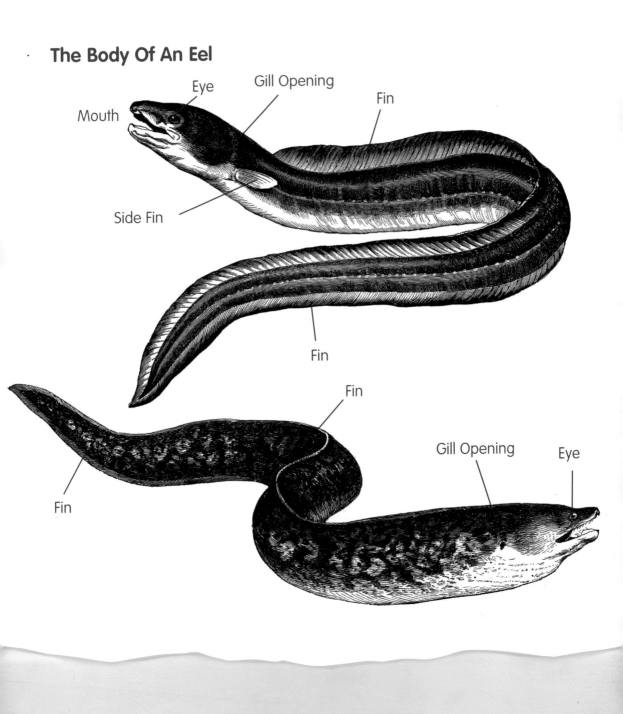

An eel generally has a single fin along its back. Some eels also have a fin on each side of their long, slender bodies.

Scientists have discovered interesting differences among eel **species**. But, there are still many eels they do not know much about.

Some eels have nostril tubes. Scientists say this feature may help eels hunt.

Other eels do not have nostril tubes.

A Growing Eel

An eel's life cycle has many stages. But for many years, scientists did not know much about it. Today, most information about the life of eels is based on a few **species**.

Eels begin life in an egg. When a young eel hatches, it floats to the ocean surface. There, it drifts with other tiny creatures called **plankton**.

FAST FACTS

Larval eels look very different from full-grown eels. For many years, scientists didn't even think they were the same kind of animal!

Next, the eel enters the larval stage. During this stage, the eel is called a leptocephalus. At this time, its body is shaped like a curly leaf.

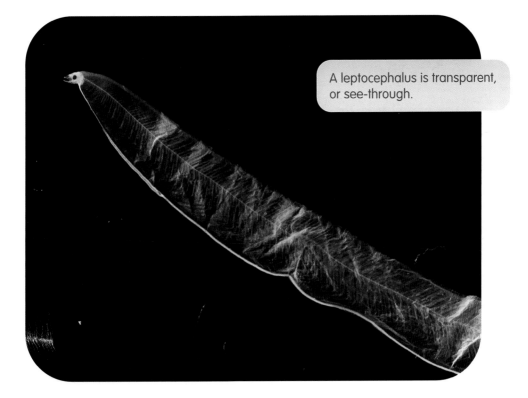

A leptocephalus is transparent, or see-through.

The leptocephalus grows as it floats in the ocean. Its body remains transparent, but it changes into a snake shape. At this stage, the tiny creature is called a glass eel.

Saltwater glass eels drift with ocean **currents**. Freshwater glass eels **migrate** toward the mouths of the rivers they live in.

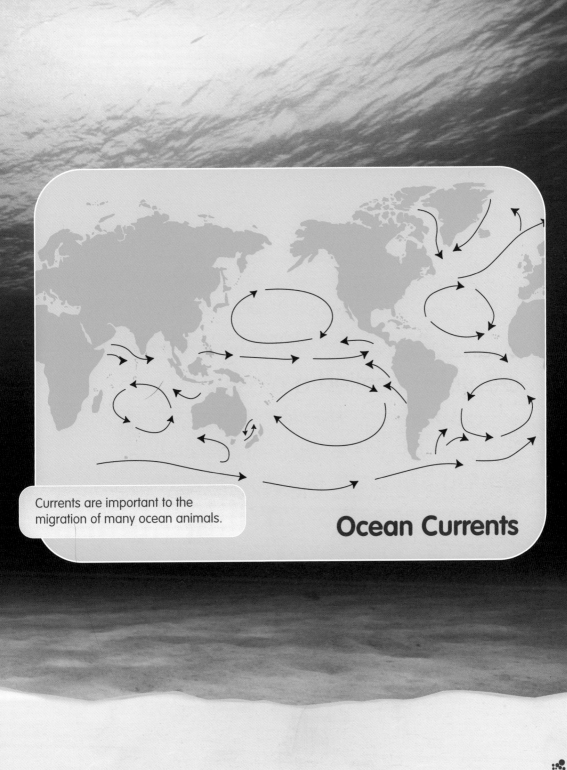

Currents are important to the
migration of many ocean animals.

Ocean Currents

Getting Stronger

As glass eels continue to grow, their bodies become colored. At this stage, the glass eels are called elvers.

Many eels remain in the ocean for their entire lives. But others travel. During the elver stage, female freshwater eels swim up rivers and streams. Some even swim up waterfalls and dams!

Female freshwater eels remain in their river **habitats** for several years. Over time, they turn a yellow green color and become yellow eels.

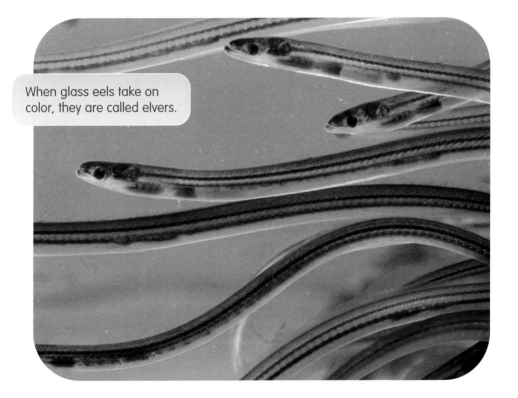

When glass eels take on color, they are called elvers.

A yellow eel's body changes one last time. Its skin turns silver, and its eyes grow larger. When this happens, the eel is an adult. It is called a silver eel.

Female freshwater silver eels return to the ocean. As adults, they are ready to lay eggs of their own. They will spend the rest of their lives in the ocean.

The water gets cloudy when an adult female eel releases her eggs.

Eel Impostors

Certain animals are confused with true eels. Many even have the word "eel" in their names. But, some are not even in the eel family!

One of the most famous impostors is the electric eel. These fish are actually related to carp. But, because of their appearance, they have adopted the eel name.

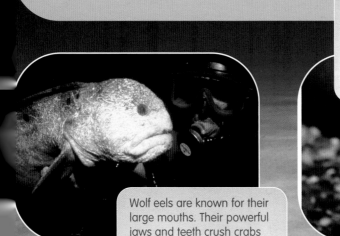

Electric eels are found in freshwater lakes and rivers in South America. These fish can produce an electric shock of about 600 volts!

Wolf eels are known for their large mouths. Their powerful jaws and teeth crush crabs and other animals.

Wolf eels are another impostor. They have long, snakelike bodies and large heads. But they are not related to eels. Slime eels, or hagfish, also resemble eels. They have very slimy skin and no fins. Some have very small eyes. Others have no eyes at all.

Hagfish produce large amounts of slimy mucus. It is slippery, like grease, and helps them escape from predators.

Hagfish can scrape the slime off their own bodies. To do this, they tie themselves into tight knots. Then, they slide the knot down toward their tail end.

The Real McCoy

A great variety of true eels are swimming in the world's oceans and rivers. Some of the most well-known eel **species** include moray, freshwater, garden, conger, and snake eels.

Freshwater eels spend part of their lives in the ocean and part in freshwater rivers and streams. They are an important food source for humans. But in some areas, overfishing is a concern.

Morays come in a wide variety of colors and patterns. Some blend into their surroundings, while others have brightly colored skin. Their mouths often hang open, allowing water to move over their gills.

Conger eels can grow up to nine feet (3 m) long and weigh more than 100 pounds (45 kg). These eels have good appetites and grow quickly!

Garden eels live in large groups at the bottom of the ocean. These small eels use their sharp tails to dig into sand. They mix skin mucus with sand to create burrows. Some garden eels won't even leave their burrows to eat! And when predators come near, they close their burrow opening with mucus.

Snake eels have sharp tips on their tails. These tips help them burrow into sand.

Dinner Hour

Eels are **carnivores**. They feed on many different types of animals. Some eat fish, while others eat shrimp. Still other eels eat **plankton** or crabs.

Moray eels feed on mollusks, such as octopuses. Freshwater eels eat fish, snails, and worms. Conger eels eat almost anything!

Many eels eat shrimp (*above left*), octopuses (*above*), and snails (*left*).

Enemy Territory

The world's waters are unsafe for leptocephaluses. **Plankton** eaters feed on these tiny creatures drifting in the ocean.

As eels grow, people also pose a **threat** to their survival. Throughout the world, many humans eat eels. Because of this, overfishing is a threat.

People also build dams in rivers that feed into the ocean. These dams make it difficult for freshwater eels to travel upstream. Some scientists are working to make sure dams do not hurt eels.

It is difficult for eels to swim over river dams. But, they are strong swimmers. Each year, some eels make it past the dams.

Fascinating Facts

Dragon eels have long, hornlike nostrils that rise above their head.

☞ Like most animals, dragon eels are born either male or female. But, females can change into males if there aren't enough males around.

☞ The world's longest eel is called the giant moray. It can grow to lengths of 12 feet (4 m) or more!

☞ In some eel **species**, males and females look nothing alike. For example, the male ribbon eel is bright blue with a yellow face and yellow fins. The female is yellow with black fins.

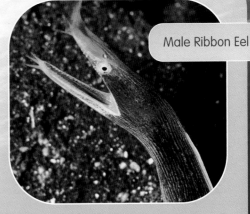

Male Ribbon Eel

☞ To tear flesh from their prey, some eels clamp down their jaws. Then, they spin around several times. This is similar to an alligator's "death roll."

☞ In Japan, cooked freshwater eel is known as *unadon*. It is a popular and expensive dish.

Learn And Explore

Until recently, scientists could only guess what life is like at the bottom of the ocean. Today's **technology** is helping them develop deep-sea **submersibles** to find out.

With these, scientists are able to study deep-sea creatures in their natural **habitats**. One such animal is the gulper eel. This very strange eel lives 3,000 to 6,000 feet (900 to 1,800 m) below the ocean's surface!

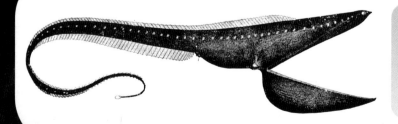

Unlike most eels, the gulper' body is not muscular. Its mo makes up about one-quarte its body length. The gulper's opens so wide that it can e animal as big as itself!

IMPORTANT WORDS

carnivore a meat-eater.

current the flow and movement of a large body of water.

habitat where an animal lives in the wild.

migrate to travel from one place to another, commonly to find food or mates.

plankton a group of very small plants and animals that float in the water. Many animals eat plankton.

species living things that are very much alike.

submersible a watercraft designed to move underwater.

technology application of scientific knowledge for practical purposes. Machines and computers were developed from such information.

threat a source of danger.

WEB SITES

To learn more about eels, visit ABDO Publishing Company on the World Wide Web. Web sites about eels are featured on our Book Links page. These links are routinely monitored and updated to provide the most current information available.

www.abdopublishing.com

INDEX

color **5, 16, 17, 18, 22, 29**

conger eel **8, 22, 23, 24**

deep-sea submersibles **30**

dragon eel **28**

eggs **12, 18, 19**

electric eel **20**

elver **16, 17**

eyes **9, 18**

fins **9, 10, 29**

food **24, 25**

freshwater eel **6, 8, 14, 16, 17, 18, 22, 24, 26, 29**

garden eel **8, 22, 23**

giant moray **28**

gills **9, 22**

glass eel **14, 16, 17**

gulper eel **30**

hagfish **18, 21**

Japan **29**

leptocephalus **13, 14, 26**

life cycle **12, 13, 14, 16, 17, 18**

moray eel **8, 22, 24**

mouth **9, 22, 30**

nostrils **11, 28**

plankton **12, 24, 26**

reproduction **12, 18, 19**

ribbon eel **29**

silver eel **18**

skin **6, 8, 18, 22, 23**

snake eel **8, 22, 23**

wolf eel **20, 21**

yellow eel **17, 18**